STORM CHASERS

On the Trail of Deadly Tornadoes

By Matt White

Reading Consultant:
Timothy Rasinski, Ph.D.
Professor of Reading Education
Kent State University

Content Consultant:
Dr. Charles A. Doswell, III
Senior Research Scientist
Cooperative Institute for
Mesoscale Meteorological Studies
University of Oklahoma

Red Brick™ Learning

Published by Red Brick™ Learning
7825 Telegraph Road, Bloomington, Minnesota 55438
http://www.redbricklearning.com

Copyright © 2003 Red Brick™ Learning. All rights reserved.

Library of Congress Cataloging-in-Publication Data
White, Matt, 1955–
    Storm chasers: on the trail of deadly tornadoes/by Matt White; reading
consultant, Timothy Rasinski.
    p. cm.—(High five reading)
    Includes bibliographic references (p. 46) and index.
    Summary: Examines what a storm chaser is and how storm chasers track,
observe, and document deadly weather, especially tornadoes, and discusses how
severe weather develops and safety precautions to take in such storms.
    ISBN 0-7368-9530-2 (Paperback)—ISBN 0-7368-9552-3 (Hardcover)
    1. Tornadoes—Juvenile literature. 2. Meteorologists—Juvenile
literature. [1. Tornadoes.] I. Title. II. Series.
QC955.2 .W47 2002
551.55'3—dc21
                         2002000189

Created by Kent Publishing Services, Inc.
Executive Editor: Robbie Butler
Designed by Signature Design Group, Inc.
This publisher has made every effort to trace ownership of all copyrighted
material and to secure necessary permissions. In the event of any questions
arising as to the use of any material, the publisher, while expressing regret for
any inadvertent error, will be happy to make necessary corrections.

Photo Credits:
Page 4, Gary Braasch/Corbis; pages 7, 12, 37, Warren Faidly/Weatherstock;
cover inset, page 9, Jim Zuckerman/Corbis; cover, pages 11, 15, 18 (top),
23, 28, 31, 33, Jim Reed/Jim Reed Photography; pages 18 (bottom), 34,
Annie Griffiths Bell/Corbis; page 25, AFP/Corbis; page 26,
Jeff Albertson/Corbis; page 39, Reuters/New Media/Inc.

No part of this book may be reproduced without written permission from the
publisher. The publisher takes no responsibility for the use of any of the materials
or methods described in this book, nor for the products thereof.

Printed in the United States of America.

3 4 5 6 08 07 06 05 04 03

Table of Contents

— CHAPTER **1** —

The Chase

What is it like to be close to a tornado? Does the wind roar? Does the ground shake? Would you like to get close to a tornado? Then maybe you would like to be a storm chaser.

Storm chasers like to get close to really bad weather. They even like to get close to killer storms. Why? Because storm chasers like to study storms.

How do storm chasers find killer storms? They use computers to gather **data** about where storms might be. Once storm chasers find a storm, they head straight for it.

Storm chasers need to be very careful around storms. Storms can change direction quickly. Storm chasers better be ready to get out of the way!

data: facts

Pack the Gear and Go!

The National Weather Service (NWS) **predicts** bad weather in Oklahoma. There may even be tornadoes. Let's follow some storm chasers.

The team makes a last-minute check. One calls out the gear. Another checks it off on a list.

"Cameras?"

"Check."

"Radios?"

"Check."

"Cellphones?"

"We've got two."

"**Satellite navigation kit**?"

"Check."

"How about the laptop computers?"

"Check."

---

predict: to guess or forecast
satellite navigation kit: tools that use a signal sent from space to find a location on Earth

Storm chasers need the right gear to do their work safely. The gear check must be carefully done. After it is complete, the storm chasers are ready to go.

They race toward the thunderstorm. The storm **lashes** at them as they approach. Will they find a tornado?

Tornado Chasing Gear Checklist
- ✓ cameras to record the storm
- ✓ radios to keep people in contact
- ✓ cellphones in case radios don't work
- ✓ satellite navigation system to map exact storm location
- ✓ laptop computers to track weather on the Internet

lash: to strike or hit

Tornado Ahead!

The storm chasers watch the sky. Ahead they see a huge **bank** of dark clouds. They're driving straight for the clouds. Rain beats down as the storm chasers get closer.

Storm chasers see the cloud base spinning fast. This is a sure sign a tornado may develop. The storm chasers stop. They set up cameras to record the action. They must act quickly.

The wind gets stronger and stronger. A **funnel-shaped** cloud appears from the cloud base. This funnel cloud grows longer. The spinning wind hits the ground. It's now a tornado.

The storm chasers take pictures and videos. Strong winds batter the crew. In the distance, the tornado hits a power line. Sparks fly as the tornado rips the pole from the ground. Then the tornado **uproots** a tree.

---

bank: a large or long mound or row
funnel-shaped: shaped like a cone, wide at the top and narrow at the bottom
uproot: to pull out by the roots

A funnel cloud touches down on a farm.

The Tornado Turns

The storm chasers get great pictures. Their cameras record the tornado as it crosses farmland. They hear the roar, like a train pounding down the tracks. They can feel a **rumbling** under their feet.

Then the tornado stops. It looks as if it's getting bigger. But wait! It only looks bigger because the tornado is heading straight for them!

The crew acts fast. They know that tornadoes are **unpredictable.** That's why they made plans ahead. They know what to do when the tornado changes direction.

Some people chase storms for a hobby. Others chase storms for their work. What kind of work do you think these **professional** storm chasers do?

---

rumbling: a deep, heavy, rolling sound
unpredictable: likely to do anything
professional: someone who is paid to do a job that takes special training

A tornado crosses farmland.

*Storm chasers and
spotters in action*

— CHAPTER **2** —

What Is a Storm Chaser?

Are you afraid of bad storms? Storm chasers aren't. In fact, they like bad weather. Storm chasers head straight for bad storms. They want to record and study them.

When bad weather **develops**, storm chasers are ready to go. They head out in cars and trucks to find a storm. Storm chasers are often the first people to see a storm.

Sometimes a storm is **severe**. Then storm chasers call the National Weather Service (NWS). The NWS sends out a storm warning. This gives people time to prepare.

Storm chasers also take pictures of the storm. They record facts about the storm, such as the wind's speed and direction.

---

develop: to grow
severe: strong or extreme

Storm Chaser or Storm Spotter?

Some storm chasers are professionals. They may be scientists who study the weather. Or they might be TV station camera teams. TV camera teams chase storms to get good pictures for the news.

Storm chasers are not the same as storm spotters. Storm spotters are **volunteers**. They also report storms to the NWS. They help out in **emergencies**. But storm spotters don't normally drive to storms.

Most states have SKYWARN volunteers. These people collect data from storm chasers and storm spotters. Internet sites then report the data. These sites warn people if a tornado or other severe weather is coming.

---

volunteer: an unpaid worker
emergency: a sudden and dangerous situation

The red color on this radar screen shows severe storms.

A group on a storm-chasing tour wait for a storm to develop.

Storm-chasing

So you think you might want to be a storm chaser. Maybe you should try a storm-chasing **tour**. But be prepared to get wet— and even bored! You will do a lot of driving and waiting. And you may see nothing.

Storm chasers run these tours. They take you to severe weather. They also teach you about storms. If you are lucky, you might see a tornado. Don't worry. Your tour guide will keep you at a safe distance.

On storm-chasing tours, you can learn how to tell if a storm is coming. Do you know any weather signs that help predict storms?

A meteorologist gets ready to photograph storm clouds.

Midwest Tornadoes
GOES-8 1km Resolution
Channel 1 - Visible
May 4, 1999 00:15 UTC

Oklahoma City

Photos from above and below a storm

Chapter 3

Tornadoes

What causes tornadoes? What makes the winds spin around so fast? Why do tornadoes seem to jump around? What do we know about tornadoes?

Weather happens all over the world. Storms are **disturbances** in the weather. Storms can cover entire states or only a small town. Whatever their size, storms are forming and going away all the time.

Storms usually move in regular ways. That helps us to predict the weather they will produce. Sometimes our predictions are wrong, though. Smaller storms are **especially** hard to predict. Tornadoes are small compared to most storms. This makes them very hard to **forecast** or predict.

---

disturbance: something that breaks up the quiet or calm
especially: very; extremely
forecast: to predict a future event

What Makes a Tornado?

In a cloud system, high-level winds may blow one way, while low-level winds blow the other way. This makes the air spin. The spinning air may **emerge** from the clouds. Then it is called a *funnel cloud*. If the funnel cloud hits the ground, it's called a *tornado*.

A tornado sucks up dirt and other matter as it moves along. This can color the tornado. For example, a tornado may turn red if it crosses over red dirt.

Tornadoes follow the storms above them. Tornadoes usually travel at 15 to 30 miles (24 to 48 kilometers) per hour. Sometimes they stay still. Tornadoes can be between 300 feet (91 meters) and half a mile (0.8 kilometer) across. Some tornadoes last just a few minutes. Others may last more than an hour.

---

emerge: to come into view

How a Tornado is Formed

1 Tornadoes start deep within thunderclouds. Warm air rises from the ground and meets strong winds above the clouds. This causes the air to spin.

2 The spinning air picks up speed. It stretches thousands of feet up and down the clouds. A funnel of spinning air drops from the cloud.

3 Soon the funnel touches the ground. The swirling wind in the funnel is strong enough to suck up cars and lift them high into the sky.

Tornado Forecasting

The National Weather Service (NWS) gives tornado warnings on TV and radio stations. But the NWS doesn't know exactly where tornadoes will form. Tornado forecasting is hard because tornadoes act in strange ways. Tornadoes sometimes happen with little warning.

So how do you know when a tornado might start? Some weather signs give us a clue. For example, tornadoes never form on clear days. But a thunderstorm with strong winds may form a tornado.

Scientists study weather signs like these. The facts these experts gather help them to forecast what weather may happen.

Weather forecasters check a radar screen.

When Do Tornadoes Happen?

Tornadoes usually strike at certain times of the year. They most often form in late winter and in spring in the United States. Tornadoes are more likely in May than October. The map shows which states have tornadoes and when.

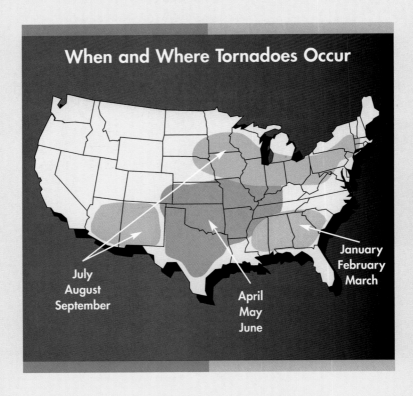

When and Where Tornadoes Occur

July
August
September

April
May
June

January
February
March

Deadly Tornadoes

The deadliest tornado to hit the United States happened in 1925. This tornado passed through Missouri, Illinois, and Indiana on March 18. It killed 695 people along its 219-mile (352-kilometer) path.

The U.S. tornado that caused the most damage hit St. Louis, Missouri in 1896. More recently, a very powerful tornado hit the Oklahoma City, Oklahoma, area on May 3, 1999.

Residents look over their damaged homes after a tornado.

Lightning is both beautiful and dangerous.

CHAPTER 4

Stay Safe

Storms are sometimes severe. Strong winds can send tree branches crashing into houses. A lightning bolt from a storm can kill you. How can you stay safe in severe weather?

Watching weather can be fun. But always remember to put safety first.

Storm chasers set a good safety example. They plan their escape **routes**. They watch weather changes at all times. They study tornadoes from a safe distance. They use their **vehicles** to escape.

But what about the rest of us? What if you are caught out in a storm? How do you hide from lightning? How do you find **shelter** from a tornado? What should you do when severe weather hits?

route: a road or path
vehicle: something in which people or goods are carried from one place to another
shelter: a safe place

Dr. Charles Doswell photographs cloud-to-ground lightning in South Dakota.

Lightning Safety

Some storms produce lightning. Lightning kills more people in the United States than any other type of weather.

Let's imagine you are caught outside in a storm. Lightning flashes all around you. Cars offer good shelter from lightning. But there are no cars nearby. What should you do?

Lightning is more likely to hit tall objects. So keep away from trees or power line poles. To be safe, crouch down on the ground. Keep your knees under you. This **posture** may look silly. But it could save your life.

---

posture: the position of your body

Stay Safe Indoors

You may be indoors when a tornado hits. If so, you need to think fast. If your house has a basement, take shelter there. Below ground is the best place to be.

What if your house has no basement? Stay on the ground floor. Keep away from windows. If glass breaks, it can harm you. An **interior** room with no windows is best.

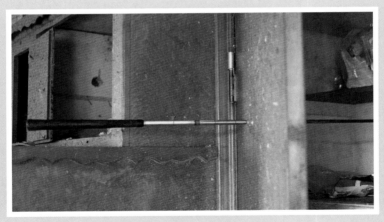

The force of a tornado shot a golf club shaft through this wooden door.

interior: the inside of something, especially a building

Tornado winds can carry flying **debris.** Debris can break through your house walls. Try to keep as many walls as possible between you and the outside.

---

debris: the remains of something broken

A piece of lumber from a house smashed the windshield.

What to Do Outdoors?

Do not be outdoors when bad weather hits. Pay attention to radio, TV, and Internet storm reports. Stay inside if severe storms are forecasted.

But what if you are caught outside in a severe storm? What if a tornado is heading your way? The best plan is to get out of the path of the tornado quickly.

If you can't escape, the best thing to do is take shelter in a **ditch**. If there isn't a ditch, lie down flat on your stomach. Put your feet toward the wind. Cover your head with your hands. The wind can't push you around as much when you lie flat. This will also help to protect you from flying debris.

Do you remember our storm chasers in Chapter 1? Follow them on the trail of a deadly storm in the next chapter.

*Storm chasers use cell phones and computers to report
severe weather.*

CHAPTER 5

Storm Chasers Save Lives

Storm chasers warn people of bad storms. In this way, they help protect lives and property. Would you like to be a storm chaser one day?

The storm chasers are out on another **mission**. Their Internet weather report shows bad storms. Tornadoes could develop.

A strong **weather front** is moving toward the town of Cleo Springs. Heavy, black storm clouds lead the way. Lightning flashes from the cloud base. High winds pound the area.

The storm chasers study the weather signs and **radar** data. They make a decision. It's time to contact the National Weather Service (NWS). This is tornado weather.

---

mission: a special job or task
weather front: the leading edge of a new weather system
radar: a tool used to find the location of storms

Tornado Touchdown

From their van, the crew sees swirling clouds under the storm. One of the crew sends a message over the radio.

"This is a tornado alert. We have funnel clouds southwest of town."

At that moment, the snake-like funnel cloud touches down. As it does, a dust cloud flies up.

"We've got a tornado here. It's heading northeast. Looks like Cleo Springs is right in its path. We suggest you **issue** warnings at once."

The crew tunes to the local radio station. Just minutes later comes a weather warning. "The National Weather Service has issued a tornado warning for the Cleo Springs area. A tornado has been spotted southwest of Cleo Springs. People in the area should seek shelter."

---

issue: to send

Meanwhile, the storm chasers watch and film the tornado. Though moving slowly, it's very strong. The tornado shows no sign of fading. It is still a few miles from Cleo Springs. The town has about 30 minutes to prepare.

A storm chaser calls in a report about a severe storm.

Town Hit by Tornado

Suddenly, the tornado **veers** northward. It just skims the edge of Cleo Springs. The tornado rips the roofs off three houses. A power line comes down. The tornado uproots several trees and destroys a trailer home.

But no one is badly hurt. Just 30 minutes can make all the difference. People can take shelter. They can prepare for tornadoes.

From outside town, the storm chasers watch the tornado. After it **skims** Cleo Springs, the tornado fades. The crew drives into town. People are cleaning up.

Cleo Springs is lucky. This time, the storm chasers reported the tornado in time. With warning, towns can survive bad weather, even tornadoes. This town did.

---

veer: to change course suddenly
skim: to barely touch

A tornado lifted the roof off this house in Arlington, Texas.

Epilogue

Dr. Charles Doswell

Dr. Charles Doswell Talks about Tornadoes

Dr. Charles Doswell has been a storm chaser since 1972. A **meteorologist**, Dr. Doswell worked at the National Storm Center **Laboratory** in Norman, Oklahoma, for 14 years. He is now retired, but he still chases storms with other meteorologists.

---

meteorologist: a person who works in weather forecasting
laboratory: a room where scientific work is done

Dr. Doswell saw his first tornado in 1972. In an **interview** for this book he recalled that day. "We drove westward to the Oklahoma border. Then we dropped south."

"On the way, we drove through the rain and hail the storm was producing. Once we were through that, my first clearly **rotating** storm was **revealed**. I just knew it was going to produce a tornado."

Sure enough, it did. "It was a brief dust whirl seen under the funnel," Dr. Doswell said. He could not hear any noise from the tornado. "It was way too far away."

"That first tornado was a small one," Dr. Doswell said. "But it was my first ever. I was **ecstatic**!"

---

interview: a meeting at which someone is asked questions
rotating: turning around and around
reveal: to show or bring into view
ecstatic: very happy

Dr. Doswell said he chases storms to help others understand severe weather. Otherwise, "I wouldn't be doing it," he said.

Dr. Doswell said scientists need to get close to tornadoes and the storms that produce them. "How can you consider yourself an **expert** about something you have never seen?" he asked.

"Observing what goes on helps scientists to do their jobs," he said. Scientists can then work out their ideas. They can test them and change them if they need to. "This is what science does," he said.

Dr. Doswell said people have been chasing storms for at least the past 50 years.

Today, groups called "intercept teams" chase storms. These teams locate and travel to storms.

---

expert: a person who has special knowledge

Dr. Doswell was a member of one of the first intercept teams, in 1972. These teams became more and more popular as people heard about them, he said.

Storm chasing is difficult, Dr. Doswell said. Many chases never find a tornado. But sometimes you get lucky.

"It's **majestic**. It's awesome. It's powerful. It's here and then it's gone without a **trace**," Dr. Doswell said. "I never stop being amazed."

---

majestic: grand
trace: a mark, track, or sign

Glossary

bank: a large or long mound or row

data: facts

debris: the remains of something broken

develop: to grow

disturbance: something that breaks up the quiet or calm

ditch: a long, narrow channel dug in the earth

ecstatic: very happy

emerge: to come into view

emergency: a sudden and dangerous situation

especially: very; extremely

expert: a person who has special knowledge

forecast: to predict a future event

funnel-shaped: shaped like a cone, wide at the top and
    narrow at the bottom

interior: the inside of something, especially a building

interview: a meeting at which someone is asked questions

issue: to send

laboratory: a room where scientific work is done

lash: to strike or hit

majestic: grand

meteorologist: a person who works in weather forecasting

mission: a special job or task

posture: the position of your body

predict: to guess or forecast

professional: someone who is paid to do a job that takes special training

radar: a tool used to find the location of storms

reveal: to show or bring into view

rotating: turning around and around

route: a road or path

rumbling: a deep, heavy, rolling sound

satellite navigation kit: tools that use a signal sent from space to find a location on Earth

severe: strong or extreme

shelter: a safe place

skim: to barely touch

tour: a trip to look at something

trace: a mark, track, or sign

unpredictable: likely to do anything

uproot: to pull out by the roots

veer: to change course suddenly

vehicle: something in which people or goods are carried from one place to another

volunteer: an unpaid worker

weather front: the leading edge of a new weather system

Bibliography

Allaby, Michael. *Secret Worlds: Tornadoes.* New York: DK Publishing, 2001.

Allen, Jean. *Tornadoes.* Natural Disasters. Mankato, Minn.: Capstone Press, 2001.

Berger, Melvin and Gilda. *Do Tornadoes Really Twist? Questions and Answers About Tornadoes and Hurricanes.* New York: Scholastic, 2000.

Chambers, Catherine. *Tornadoes.* Disasters in Nature. Oxford: Heinemann Library, 2001.

Cosgrove, Brian. *Weather.* Eyewitness Books. New York: DK Publishing, 2000.

Green, Jen. *Closer Look at Hurricanes and Typhoons.* London: Franklin Watts, 1998.

Jennings, Terry. *Hurricanes and Tornadoes.* Natural Disasters. Mankato, Minn.: Thameside Press, 1999.

Maslin, Mark. *Storms.* Restless Planet. Texas: Raintree/Steck-Vaughn, 1999.

Useful Addresses

Meteorological Office
London Road
Bracknell
Berkshire RG12 2SZ
United Kingdom

National Weather Service
1325 East-West Highway
Silver Spring, MD 20910

Internet Sites

Chuck Doswell's Home Page
www.cimms.ou.edu/~doswell/

National Severe Storms Laboratory
www.nssl.noaa.gov/

National Weather Service
www.nws.noaa.gov/

Skywarn
www.skywarn.org/

Stormtrack
www.stormtrack.org/

Index